Edmaz Book of English Language:

Grade Four

(Revised Edition)

Published

By

Edson Mazira

ISBN 978-1-77906-388-5

Edmaz Book of English Language: Grade Four

© Edson Mazira, 2020

(Sketch drawings by Edson Mazira)

Preamble

Edmaz Book of English Language: Grade Four was written mainly for the pupils in Zimbabwe.

The book covers a few topics on the alphabet, the noun, the pronoun, the adjective, the verb, the adverb, and so on.

There are comprehensions and reading tasks to improve vocabulary.

At the end of the book, there are answers for every exercise set to test the pupils.

Acknowledgement

I grab this opportunity to thank all the veteran writers from whose books I consumed quality education. These are Shimmer Chinodya, Charles Mungoshi, S.R. Golding, Raymond Murphy, Jane Straus, Peter Herring, John Eastwood and many others.

Finally, I thank my brothers Christopher Mazira and Luckson Mazira for their support.

Contents

School holiday [Part 1]

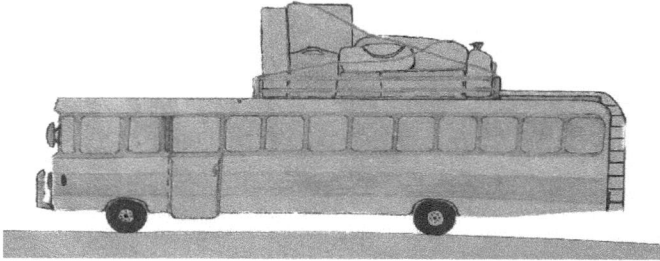

Sunday, a sunny day, was the last day on which Farisai said goodbye to the city of Harare and to her town friends. Now she was on a bus with tinted windows. She was not very happy because no one could see her from the outside. Seated on the back seat, she rehearsed silently how she was going to tell Thandiwe about the town girls, the traffic robots, the zebra crossings and the roadshows.

Within her heart, she also thanked Uncle Eddy for taking her to the city, where she had got a lot to tell her rural friends at school. Thandiwe, her neighbour, was going to be the first friend to get it all.

Some hours later, the bus reached Farisai's village. The sun had set, and there was no moon. No one was at the bus stop; that made Farisai unhappy. She had been expecting to see her friends playing there.

Exercise

1. Sunday was the_____.
   A. bus
   B. Thandiwe
   C. day on which Farisai left the city of Harare
   D. city of Harare
2. Farisai was not very happy because_____.
   A. the tinted windows made the bus look ugly

B. no one could see her from the outside

C. the bus left the city of Harare

D. she sat on the back seat

3. Farisai and Thandiwe were_____.

   A. enemies

   B. not neighbours

   C. friends

   D. town friends

4. Who did Farisai thank for taking her to the city of Harare?

   A. Harare City Council

   B. School holiday

   C. Uncle Eddy

   D. Her town friends

5. Why was Farisai unhappy when the bus reached her village?

   A. Farisai was unhappy because the bus stopped.

   B. Farisai was unhappy because no one was at the bus stop.

   C. Farisai was unhappy because her friends were playing there.

D. Farisai was unhappy because the sun had set.

The alphabet

Aa Bb Cc Dd Ee Ff Gg Hh Ii Jj Kk
Ll Mm Nn Oo Pp Qq Rr Ss Tt Uu
Vv Ww Xx Yy Zz

Consonant letters in the alphabet

Bb Cc Dd Ff Gg Hh Jj Kk Ll Mm
Nn Pp Qq Rr Ss Tt Vv Ww Xx Yy
Zz

Vowel letters in the alphabet

Aa Ee Ii Oo Uu

Exercise

1. Which word starts with a consonant letter?
   A. car   B. onion
   C. ear   D. umbrella
2. Which word starts with a vowel letter?

A. car   B. vowel

C. onion   D. consonant

3. The letter **x** is a_____letter.

A. cross   B. consonant

C. vowel   D. cancelling

4. The letter_____is a vowel letter.

A. e   B. s   C. x   D. q

5. The alphabet is made up_____.

A. of consonant letters only

B. of vowel letters only

C. of consonant letters and vowel letters

D. by the teachers

Task 1: Vocabulary

Consonant Vowel Onion	Roadshow Robots Uncle	Tinted

School holiday [Part 2]

It is the next day of Sunday. Every school will open tomorrow. Farisai is washing her school uniforms. Thandiwe is helping her. Mr Kabiseni, Farisai's grandfather, is carving a yoke. He is under a mango tree.

Farisai is telling her story about the holiday. She says, "I really enjoyed my holiday. I saw many things in Harare. My uncle taught me a lot. Now, I know what to do whenever I want to cross any traffic road."

Thandiwe asks, "What do you do when you want to cross it?"

"When I want to cross any traffic road," Farisai says, "I check first for the vehicles approaching from my right side. Secondly, I watch out for those approaching from my left side. If both sides are clear, I now cross the road.

"At a zebra crossing, as a pedestrian, I have the right to cross the road. Every vehicle must stop and give me the right of way."

"What is a zebra crossing?" Thandiwe asks.

"It's a marked way that runs across a tarred road. That's where every pedestrian has the right to cross the road. The vehicles stop and give them the right of way. But this crossing should be done with caution because some drivers are reckless; they ignore to stop at the zebra crossings," Farisai says.

"Okay," Thandiwe says.

"At the road robots," Farisai continues, "I have the right to cross the road when the robot is green. Red means I must stop!

"Everyone should always exercise caution when crossing these roads. This doesn't matter whether or not they have the right of way. They should also leave the habit of crossing the roads, whilst their eyes are focused on cellphones."

"Thank you, Farisai," Thandiwe says. "I have learnt a lot from you."

Mr Kabiseni says smilingly, "I am also pleased with you, my granddaughter."

Exercise

1. The next day of Sunday is_____.
   A. Sunday   B. Tuesday
   C. Monday   D. Friday
2. Farisai's grandfather is under_____.
   A. a gum tree
   B. a baobab tree
   C. a mango tree
   D. a pine tree
3. Pedestrians have the right to cross_____.
   A. at zebra crossings
   B. against red robots
   C. by bus
   D. whilst their eyes are focused on cellphones
4. A pedestrian is a_____.
   A. person with a cellphone
   B. traffic road
   C. zebra crossing
   D. person who walks on foot
5. When a robot turns green, it means you have the right_____.
   A. to proceed

B. to stop

C. to wash your uniforms

D. to use cellphones

Task 2: Vocabulary

Pedestrian Vehicle Carve	Yoke Caution Reckless

Nouns

A noun is a name or a naming word. There are proper nouns and common nouns.

Proper nouns always start with capital letters.

Common nouns always start with small letters, except where they start sentences.

Proper nouns	Common nouns
Edson	boy

Thandiwe	girl
Mazira	man
Sipho	woman

Common nouns in singular and plural forms

Singular form	Plural form
House	houses
Calf	calves
Goose	geese
Sheep	sheep
Woman	women
Man	men
Ox	oxen
Donkey	donkeys
Photo	photos

Potato	potatoes
Tomato	tomatoes
Boy	boys
Girl	girls
Table	tables
Plate	plates
Box	boxes
Tortoise	tortoises
Foot	feet
Tooth	teeth
Mouse	mice

Basic uses of a/an

The article **'a'** is used before a singular common noun or word that starts with a consonant sound.

The article **'an'** is used before a singular common noun or word that starts with a vowel sound.

Common nouns that start with consonant sounds	Common nouns that start with vowel sounds
a **b**ed	**an o**nion
a **g**irl	**an e**gg
a **m**an	**an a**dult
a **w**oman	**an u**mbrella
a **t**eacher	**an a**eroplane
a **d**og	**an o**range
a **n**urse	**an i**gloo

The articles **'a'** and **'an'** are not used for plural nouns.

Basic use of the

The article **'the'** is used for a common noun that is mentioned again. When it is the first time to mention the noun, we use 'a' or 'an'.

Examples:

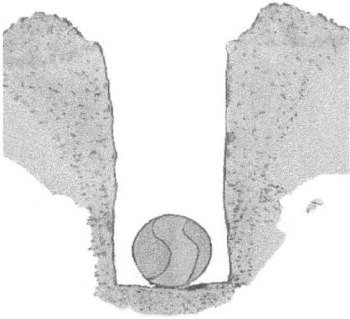

This is **a** pit. **The** pit has a ball in it. [Correct]

This is **a** pit. **A** pit has a ball in it. [Wrong]

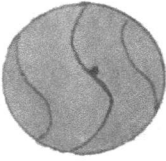

This is **a** beautiful ball. **The** ball belongs to Tinotenda Mazira. [Correct]

This is **a** beautiful ball. **A** ball belongs to Tinotenda Mazira. [Wrong]

Exercise

Answers		
the	an	a

1. This is___egg. ___egg is mine.
2. That is___baboon. ___baboon is eating a maize cob.
3. That is___orange. ___orange is on the ground.
4. That is__elephant. __elephant is feeding on tree leaves.
5. This is___dog. ___dog belongs to Mr Mvurayatota.

Sekuru Masiye Tells a Story

"Once upon a time, there were a tortoise, two eagles and three herdboys.

"One day, the tortoise woke up early in the morning and moved to a river in Chiutsi Village called Chipfungwe. He was searching for some water to drink. Unfortunately, as it was in the dry season, the river was dry. So he did not find any water. The only river that had been left with some water was Nyautande in Kapfudza Village. It was about four kilometres away from Chiutsi Village.

"That day, the weather was very hot, and the temperature increased as the sun crept towards the noontime. The tortoise starved on his way to Nyautande River.

"In the afternoon, the two eagles found the tortoise struggling. They landed to offer him some help.

"As the eagles helped the tortoise, they told him to keep his mouth shut. One eagle took a stick and gripped one end with his beak. In the same manner, the other one gripped the other end. The tortoise was told to grip the middle of the stick, and he did so. They flew east.

"As they flew over a hill, the three boys herding their cattle shouted, 'Look at that poor tortoise! It's hung on a stick like a junky piece of cloth on a line!'

"The boys went on laughing at the tortoise until he opened his mouth to answer back. When he did so, he fell down from the stick.

"The next place the tortoise found himself was on a rocky ground. His shell had broken into pieces.

"This is the end of the story. It teaches us to control our emotions," Sekuru Masiye says.

Exercise

1. At first, the tortoise went to_____.
   A. Nyautande River
   B. Chipfungwe River
   C. Kapfudza Village
   D. the eagles

2. Did the tortoise find any water in Chipfungwe River?
   A. Yes, he did.
   B. He found it.
   C. The tortoise just found a little.
   D. No, he didn't find the water.
3. How many eagles helped the tortoise?
   A. ten   B. three
   C. six   D. two
4. ____shouted at the tortoise.
   A. The eagles
   B. The middle of the stick
   C. A rocky ground
   D. The boys
5. The____of the tortoise broke into pieces.
   A. front legs
   B. shell
   C. head
   D. rear legs

Task 3: Vocabulary

Search	Unfortunately
Season	Struggle
Grip	Starve
Rocky	

Task 4: Confusing words

Piece; peace	Size; seize
Stake; steak	Node; nod
Price; prize	Advise; advice
Pouch; porch	Accept; except
Lose; loose	

1. Price; prize

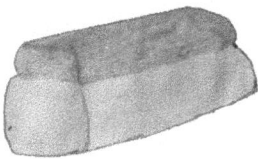

The **price** of this bread is $0.50.

My father bought me a ball as a **prize**.

2. Pouch; porch

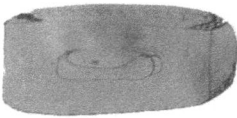

This is a **pouch** of my cellphone.

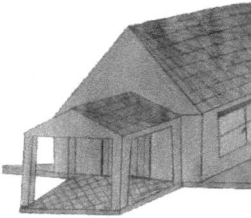

This is a **porch**. It is also known as a veranda.

3. Stake; steak

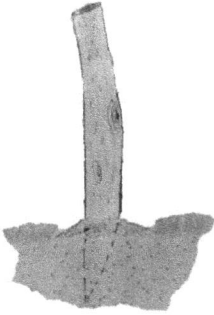

This is a **stake** of a tree.

This is a **steak** of meat.

4. Piece; peace

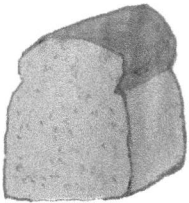

This is a **piece** of bread.

There is no **peace** in their country.

5. Node; nod

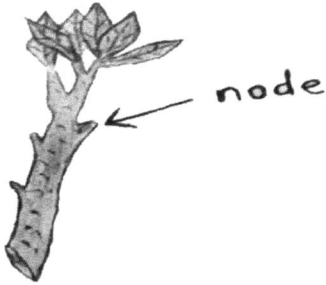

This is a **node** on a branch.

I usually **nod** my head in agreement whenever my teacher expresses a good point.

6. Size; seize

The **size** of this t-shirt is 14.

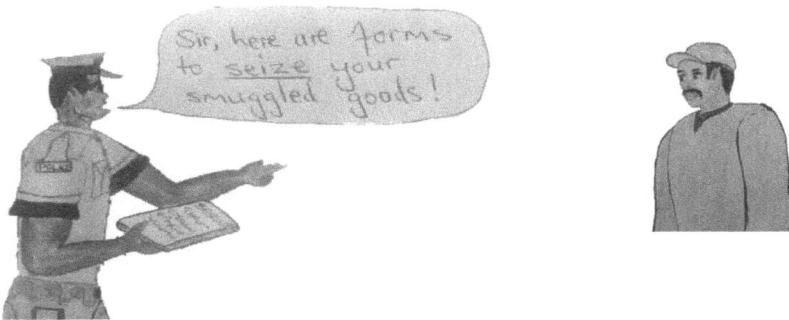

Sir, here are forms to **seize** your smuggled goods!

7. Advise; advice

Mr Bhero: I **advise** you to respect elders.

James: Thanks. I take your **advice**.

8. Lose; loose

I always **lose** the game.

This knot is **loose**.

9. Accept; except

Themba: Sir, can you **accept** me as your friend?

Mr Moyo: Yes, but **except** your dog!

Adjectives

Adjectives are words that describe people, animals or things.

Examples:

Good	Bad	Beautiful	Big
Tall	Short	Long	Clever
Foolish	Angry	Ugly	Quick
Slow	Fast	Dark	Light
Happy	Fine	Tight	Many
Much	Few	Wise	Low

Adjectives in comparison

Positive degree	Comparative degree	Superlative degree
Good	better	best
Bad	worse	worst
Tall	taller	tallest
Short	shorter	shortest
Foolish	more foolish	most foolish
Angry	angrier	angriest
Clever	cleverer	cleverest
Quick	quicker	quickest
Beautiful	more beautiful	most beautiful
Ugly	uglier	ugliest

Tall   taller   tallest

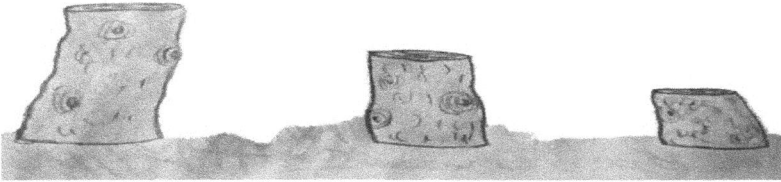

Short   shorter   shortest

How adjectives describe people, animals or things

Without an adjective	With an adjective
This is a boy.	This is a **tall** boy.
This is a girl.	This is a **beautiful** girl.

| This is an animal. | This is a **foolish** animal. |
| These are lions. | These are **angry** lions. |

Exercise

Find the missing word, and fill in the gap:

Positive degree	Comparative degree	Superlative degree
....	better	best
....	worse	....
Beautiful	....	....
Happy	....	....
New	....	....
....	faster	fastest

Many/much

We use **many** when we refer to countable things.

We use **much** when we refer to uncountable things.

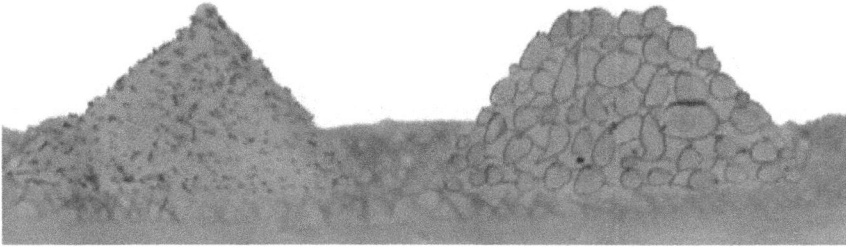

Much sand   **many** stones

Exercise

1. How_____girls visited you?
2. I need_____sand.
3. There was_____oil in the tank.
4. I saw_____donkeys on his farm.
5. There is_____rain in this season.

This/that

This and **that** are used to indicate people, animals or things (in singular forms).

Examples:

1. **This car** is new. [Correct]
   This cars are new. [Wrong]

2. **That car** is new. [Correct]
   That cars are new. [Wrong]

This shirt is cheap.

That shirt is cheap.

This indicates:	Examples:
- A person, an animal or a thing that we are in contact with.	- **This** ruler is yours. - **This** cow is fat. - **This** book is new.
- A place or a	- **This** country is

situation within which we are.	mine. - **This** economy is changing. - **This** situation is tough.

That indicates:	Examples:
- A person, an animal or a thing that we are not in contact with.	- **That** car is yours. - **That** cow is fat. - **That** book is new.
- A place or a situation within which we are not.	- **That** country is mine. - **That** economy is changing. - **That** situation is tough.

These/those

These and **those** are the plural forms of **this** and **that**, respectively. They are used to indicate people, animals or things that are in plural forms.

Examples:

1. **These balls** are beautiful. [Correct]
   These ball is beautiful. [Wrong]

2. **Those cows** belong to Patson. [Correct]
   Those cow belongs to Patson. [Wrong]

These balls are mine.

Those balls are mine.

These indicates:	Examples:

- People, animals or things that we are in contact with.	- **These** people are clever. - **These** books are new. - **These** cattle are fat.
- Places or situations within which we are.	- **These** countries are in Africa. - **These** situations are tough.

Those indicates:	Examples:
- People, animals or things that we are not in contact with.	- **Those** plans failed. - **Those** houses are far away from us. - **Those** people are our friends.
- Places or situations within which we are not.	- **Those** countries are in Africa. - **Those** situations were tough.

Exercise

1. _____sheep are fat.
   A. This   B. That
   C. These   D. Much
2. _____sheep usually grazes alone.
   A. Those   B. These
   C. That   D. Many
3. _____boy is wise.
   A. These   B. This
   C. Those   D. Them
4.

_____ball is mine.

   A. This   B. Those
   C. These   D. That
5.

_____suit I am wearing is not mine.

A. This   B. That
C. These   D. Those

Pronouns

Pronouns are words that replace nouns.

1.

John is tall.

He is tall.

2. May you hand this pen over to **John**?

May you hand this pen over to **him**?

3.

Thandiwe is short.

She is short.

4. I asked **Thandiwe**.

I asked **her**.

5.

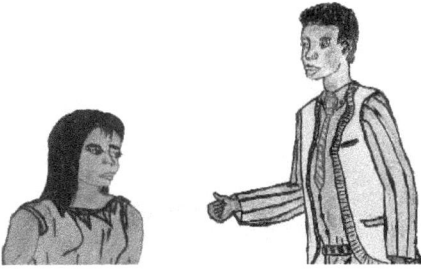

Thandiwe and **John** are friends.

They are friends.

6.

These bags belong to **John** and **Thandiwe**.

These bags belong to **them**.

7.

Edson killed the **snake**.

Edson killed **it**.

8. A **snake** is a dangerous animal.

   It is a dangerous animal.

Exercise

Replace the underlined noun(s) with a suitable pronoun from the answer box:

Answers				
he	him	they	she	it
her	them			

1. Our <u>teachers</u> are smart.
2. <u>Rudo</u> is my sister.
3. I kicked the <u>ball</u>.
4. May you send this message to <u>Mary and Sipho</u>?
5. I gave <u>Peter</u> a new pen.

6. A <u>parrot</u> is a clever bird.

7. She ate all the <u>rice</u>.

8. To <u>Grace</u>, give my regards.

9. These <u>oxen</u> belong to Mr Chinua.

10.   <u>Sam Andrew</u> is a soldier.

Dialogue: Simon and Rudo

Simon: Hey, Rudo! What'll you be doing tomorrow?

Rudo: I'll be doing some house chores. What about you?

Simon: I'll be herding my grandpa's cattle.

Rudo: That's good. We need to help our families.

Simon: Not only our families—

Rudo: That's right; we also need to help the whole community.

Simon: Yes.

Rudo: Goodbye, Simon. See you on Monday. Have a good weekend.

Simon: Thank you, Rudo.

Exercise

1. Simon is talking with_____.
   A. Dialogue
   B. Rudo
   C. his grandpa's cattle
   D. his community
2. Who will be doing some house chores?
   A. Simon   B. Dialogue
   C. No one   D. Rudo

3. _____will be herding his grandpa's cattle.

   A. Simon's grandpa

   B. Rudo

   C. Simon

   D. Simon with Rudo

4. Simon and Rudo are_____.

   A. friends   B. puppies

   C. duties   D. cattle

5. Rudo promises to meet Simon_____.

   A. on Thursday

   B. on Monday

   C. on Friday

   D. on Sunday

Prepositions

Examples (of prepositions):

in	under	on	between
beneath	among		behind

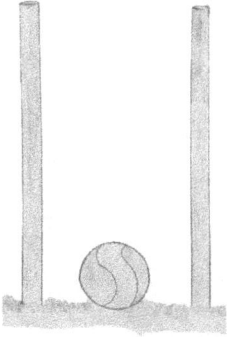

The ball is **between** two poles.

The ball is **on** a stool.

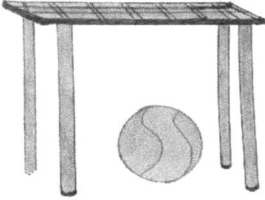

The ball is **under** a stool.

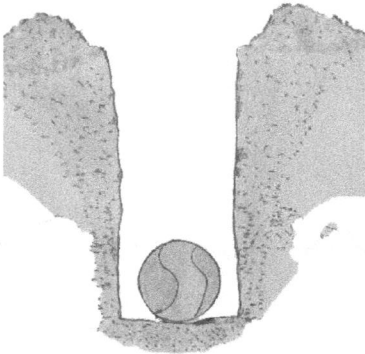

The ball is **in** a pit.

Task 5: Homework

Find more than ten prepositions, and use them in your own sentences.

Verbs

A verb is a doing word. It is a word that shows action or state of being.

Examples (of verbs):

Be	Walk	Do
Write	Sing	Win
Drive	Jump	Speak
Talk	Raise	Sleep
Come	See	Eat
Draw	Dance	Show
Run	Die	Rise
Listen	Tell	Cut

Verbs in various tenses

Present simple tense

This is when the action happens regularly in the present time.

1. Jane **goes** to school **every day**.
2. Jane and John **go** to school **every day**.

3. They **go** to school **every day**.
4. I **go** to school **every day**.
5. We **go** to school **every day**.

Past simple tense

This is when the action happened in the past.

1. She **visited** her sister **last year**.
2. I **talked** about it **yesterday**.
3. **Last week**, she **bought** a nice car.
4. Edson **killed** a snake.
5. They **came** here **last month**.

Present progressive tense

This is when the action is happening **continuously** in the present time. This form is also known as the present continuous tense. In this way, the verbs end in '-ing'.

1. I **am talking** to Tinashe Mazira.
2. They **are running**.
3. She **is driving** her car.

4. James **is doing** his work.
5. The dog **is dying**.

Past continuous tense

This is when the action was happening **continuously** in the past. The verbs end in '-ing'.

1. I **was talking** to Tinashe Mazira.
2. They **were running**.
3. She **was driving** her car.
4. James **was doing** his work.
5. The dog **was dying**.

Future simple tense

This is when the action will happen in the future.

1. I **shall remind** you tomorrow.
2. She **will drive** her car.
3. James **will do** his work.
4. We **shall let** you come with us.
5. They **will share** it.

Future continuous tense

This is when the action will be happening continuously in the future. In this case, the verbs end in '-ing'.

1. I **shall be reminding** you after every hour.
2. She **will be driving** her car after every two days.
3. James **will be doing** his work.
4. We **shall be informing** you of every change.
5. They **will be sharing** it.

Regular verbs

Regular verbs end in '-ed' or '-d' when they are put into their past tense.

Examples (of regular verbs):

Bare infinitive	Past tense
Talk	talked
Walk	walked
Kill	killed

Kick	kicked
Dance	danced
Listen	listened
Move	moved
Pay	paid
Play	played
Die	died

Irregular verbs

Irregular verbs end in an irregular way when they are put into their past tense.

Examples (of irregular verbs):

Bare infinitive	Past tense
Go	went
Come	came

Sing	sang
Do	did
See	saw
Speak	spoke
Win	won
Draw	drew
Become	became
Dig	dag
Quit	quit
Beat	beat

Modal verbs

Modal verbs are helping verbs. They help the main verbs.

Auxiliary verbs

Like the modal verbs, auxiliary verbs also are helping verbs. They also help the main verbs.

Examples (of modal verbs, auxiliary verbs and main verbs):

Modal verbs	Auxiliary verbs	Main verbs
Can	Do	Go
Could		Drive
Shall		Walk
	Be	
Should		Jump
Will		Sing
Would	Have	See

Exercise

1. I_____him yesterday.

   A. see   B. saw

   C. sees   D. seeing

2. They are_____today.

   A. comes   B. came

   C. come   D. coming

3. The past tense of buy is_____.

   A. buyed   B. buying

   C. buys   D. bought

4. She will_____next week.

   A. go   B. goes

   C. going   D. went

5. Simba and Farisai_____every day before they sleep.

   A. prays   B. prayed

   C. praying   D. pray

6. The team will be_____tomorrow.

   A. playing   B. play

   C. plays   D. played

7. Except_____, the following words are modal verbs.

   A. could   B. can

   C. would   D. be

8. Except____, the following words are main verbs.

    A. walk   B. can

    C. die   D. sleep

9. The past tense of *be* is____.

    A. beed   B. bed

    C. was   D. been

10.   Fill in the gaps:

Bare infinitive	Past tense
Ring	....
....	slept
....	picked
Shake	....
....	dried
Bear	....
....	sat
....	ate
Weep	....
Jump	....

The adventure:

Makaro [Part 1]

In the village of Nyamagweta lived a greedy man called Makaro. He was a giant-but-lazy man.

Makaro chased away his family so that he could cook and eat everything alone. He slaughtered all his domestic animals for meat. When the animals were all finished, he began to steal from his neighbours.

One night, he stole a goat from a wrong person's kraal. Right there, he saw two big human heads with no bodies. The heads called him by his name. Makaro dropped the goat and ran away.

In a nearby forest, he found a hollow in a baobab tree. No sooner had he crawled into the hollow than the two heads reached the place and left a coffin near the entrance.

Makaro fainted.

Exercise

1. Makaro lived in the village of_____.
   A. Chiutsi
   B. Kapfudza
   C. Nyamagweta
   D. Katarira
2. Makaro was_____.
   A. thin   B. not greedy
   C. barren   D. lazy
3. How many heads did Makaro see?
   A. two
   B. four
   C. six
   D. eight

4. The heads left_____near the entrance.

    A. a goat

    B. a wrong person's kraal

    C. a hollow in a baobab tree

    D. a coffin

5. What happened to Makaro after the heads had left the coffin?

    A. Makaro beat them

    B. The heads sang for him

    C. Makaro fainted

    D. Makaro chased them away

Task 6: Vocabulary

Greediness	Neighbour
Entrance	Kraal
Slaughter	Coffin

Adverbs

Adverbs are words that modify verbs, adjectives or other adverbs.

Examples (of adverbs):

Slowly	Smilingly
Quickly	Sadly
Happily	Wisely
Foolishly	Beautifully

1. The tortoise **moved slowly**.
2. The walls were **beautifully painted**.

In number 1, **slowly** modifies **moved**. In number 2, **beautifully** modifies **painted**.

Task 7: Homework

Find fifteen adverbs other than these given above.

Correlatives

Correlatives are certain words that usually work together.

Either *with* **or**

Either works with **or**.

1. **Either** Tinotenda **or** Patson will do the work.

Neither *with* **nor**

Neither works with **nor**.

1. **Neither** Tinotenda **nor** Patson will do the work.

Exercise

1. _____Sam **nor** Maidei is a teacher.
   A. Either   B. So
   C. Neither   D. That
2. **Either** you_____your sister is going to win it.
   A. or   B. nor
   C. that   D. but

Punctuation

Punctuation marks:

Mark	Name

?	Question mark
!	Exclamation mark
.	Period (or full stop)
,	Comma
"	Opening inverted commas
"	Closing inverted commas
'	Apostrophe

The adventure:

Makaro [Part 2]

When Makaro woke up, the coffin had disappeared. He crawled out of the hollow and went home.

One day, he went hunting. In the forest, he found a water place with many birds. There, he set his traps and went away.

After two hours, he came back to check the traps. There were many birds around the place, but they all flew away. Someone had tempered with his traps.

Makaro was angry. He set the traps again and went home.

The following day, it happened again, and it continued to happen the same way.

One afternoon, Makaro made an

ambush. He climbed up a tall tree, which was near the place, and hid within its leafy branches.

Within a few minutes, a tall human skeleton arrived and shouted angrily, "Who's this culprit disturbing my traps? It's too much now! I have to get them today!" It staggered towards the tree on which Makaro was and sat down. Its back leaned against the trunk.

Some fear attacked the greedy hunter, and he began to pass some urine, which spattered on the head of the skeleton.

The skeleton said, "It's raining."

Exercise

1. When Makaro woke up,___had disappeared.

   A. the hollow

   B. the birds

   C. the coffin

   D. the traps

2. Why did Makaro set the traps?

   A. Makaro set the traps because he wanted to catch some fish.

   B. Makaro set the traps because he wanted to catch the skeleton.

   C. Makaro set the traps because he wanted to catch the birds.

   D. Makaro set the traps because he wanted to catch nothing.

3. Did Makaro catch any bird?

   A. No, he didn't.

   B. Yes, he did.

C. He caught just one bird.

D. He caught the skeleton.

4. Why did Makaro pass some urine?

A. Makaro passed some urine because the traps had caught no bird.

B. Makaro passed some urine because the skeleton had told him to do so.

C. Makaro passed some urine because he had found a toilet.

D. Makaro passed some urine because he was afraid of the skeleton.

5. The skeleton thought the urine was_____.

A. Makaro's urine

B. some dew

C. some rain

D. river water

Task 8: Vocabulary

Spatter	Disappear	Stagger
Climb	Ambush	Culprit

Task 9: Vocabulary

Making use of the vowels given in the box, fill in the gaps with your own words of less than three consonants:

Vowels	Words
-a-	e.g. hat
-a-	....
-a-	....
-a-	....
-a-	....
-a-	....
-ea-	e.g. beat
-ea-	....
-ea-	....
-ea-	....

-ea-	....
-ea-	....
-i-	e.g. hit
-i-	....
-i-	....
-i-	....
-i-	....
-i-	....
-o-	e.g. hot
-o-	....
-o-	....
-o-	....
-o-	....
-o-	....
-oo-	e.g. loot
-oo-	....
-oo-	....
-oo-	....
-oo-	....
-oo-	....
-u-	e.g. hut
-u-	....
-u-	....
-u-	....
-u-	....
-u-	....

The adventure:

Makaro [Part 3]

Makaro fell off the tree and bumped on the skeleton, which got up and sprinted east. At the same time, the man got up and took the opposite direction.

As the skeleton was running, it saw people's houses in front of it and made a quick U-turn. Makaro almost did the same; he caught sight of some graves and made a quick U-turn, too.

The two met at a sharp corner and hit each other. Both of them fainted.

Some minutes later, Makaro woke up first and ran away. When the skeleton woke up, it didn't see what had knocked it down. It left the place and went to the graveyard.

From that day, Makaro became a changed man.

Exercise

1. Makaro fell_____.

   A. onto the tree

B. onto the skeleton

C. onto the traps

D. onto the trunk

2. _____got up and sprinted east.

   A. Makaro   B. Nobody

   C. The skeleton   D. The tree

3. A graveyard is a place where_____.

   A. grapes are planted

   B. people live

   C. Makaro set his traps

   D. the dead are buried

4. Where did Makaro and the skeleton hit each other?

   A. Makaro and the skeleton hit each other in a river.

   B. Makaro and the skeleton hit each other at a sharp corner.

   C. Makaro and the skeleton hit

each other at the graveyard.

D. Makaro and the skeleton did not hit each other.

5. Did Makaro become a changed man?

A. Makaro never changed his behaviour.

B. No, he didn't become a changed man.

C. He didn't do that.

D. Yes, he became a changed man.

Task 10: Vocabulary

Opposite Bump	Faint Graveyard	Knock U-turn

Build Zimbabwe

We are our future country.
If you build us,
You build Zimbabwe.

Our education
Is our future country.
If you build it,
You build Zimbabwe.

Our health
Is our future country.
If you build it,
You build Zimbabwe.

Our rights
Are our future country.
If you consider them,
You build Zimbabwe.

Our voice
Is our future country.
If you hear it,
You build Zimbabwe.

All the children
Are our future country.
If you build them,
You build Zimbabwe.

(By Edson Mazira)

Task 11: Poem

1. Recite the poem, Build Zimbabwe.

Answers

School holiday [Part 1]:

1. C   2. B   3. C   4. C   5. B

The alphabet *(vowels and consonants)*:

1. A   2. C   3. B   4. A   5. C

School holiday [Part 2]:

1. C   2. C   3. A   4. D   5. A

Nouns *(and the articles)*:

1. an; the   2. a; the

3. an; the   4. an; the

5. a; the

Sekuru Masiye Tells a Story:

1. B   2. D   3. D   4. D   5. B

Adjectives:

Positive degree	Comparative degree	Superlative degree
Good	better	best
Bad	worse	worst
Handsome	more handsome	most handsome
Happy	happier	happiest
New	newer	newest
Fast	Faster	Fastest

Many/much:

1. Many   2. Much   3. Much

4. Many   5. Much

This/that *and* these/those:

1. C   2. C   3. B   4. D   5. A

Pronouns:

1. They   2. She   3. It   4. Them

5. Him   6. It   7. It   8. Her

9. They   10. He

Dialogue: Simon and Rudo:

1. B   2. D   3. C   4. A   5. B

Verbs:

1. B   2. D   3. D   4. A   5. D

6. A   7. D   8. B   9. C

10.

Bare infinitive	Past tense
Ring	rang
Sleep	slept
Pick	picked
Shake	shook
Dry	dried

Bear	bore
Sit	sat
Eat	ate
Weep	wept
Jump	jumped

The adventure: Makaro [Part 1]:

1. C   2. D   3. A   4. D   5. C

Correlatives:

1. C   2. A

The adventure: Makaro [Part 2]:

1. C   2. C   3. A   4. D   5. C

The adventure: Makaro [Part 3]:

1. B   2. C   3. D   4. B   5. D

Index

www.ingramcontent.com/pod-product-compliance
Lightning Source LLC
Chambersburg PA
CBHW060529030426
42337CB00021B/4200